It was Valentine's Day! George and his friend invited the neighborhood kids over to celebrate. George was so excited.

First George and his friends
decorated the house.

George loves balloons.

How big could his get?

Big . . . **Bigger** . . .

Then they decorated cookies. There were three colors of icing and many different kinds of sprinkles.

The icing looked nice
on George's cookie . . .

Now what would they do next? Make valentines, of course! George made a special card for the man with the yellow hat.

That big box was certainly very interesting.

Perhaps he could create something with it.

George thought and thought.

Then George had an idea.
He put a bow here and
some glitter there, then cut
a hole in the top.

George was making . . .

Everyone began to clean up.

Before he knew it, all that
hard work made George a
sleepy monkey.